Buddy the Beagle on Blueberry Street

To Shannon,
Buddy speaks to all who listen.
Debbie Burton

Endorsements

I fell in love with Buddy who stars in Debbie Burton's latest children's story, *Buddy the Beagle on Blueberry Street*. Buddy, who ends up with his back legs paralyzed following an accident, faces every challenge with great courage, and his example will inspire readers of every age—especially children. This story also emphasizes the importance of love and a supportive family in times of crisis. As someone who has served on the board of our local Humane Society, I've always loved dogs. They teach us how to love unconditionally, and they inspire us to be better people. I truly believe Buddy's story will have that same effect on readers.
—**Michelle Medlock Adams**, Award-winning Journalist & Bestselling Author of more than 80 books.

Any dog lover, young or old, will be able to relate to this heartwarming story about an injured dog and his road to recovery. Ms. Burton shares this real-life adventure with passion and humor, while showing her readers that perseverance, kindness, and love can win the day!
—**Dr. Randall Hart**, Principal, Dover Shores Elementary

Buddy the beagle always keeps his great outlook on life. His priorities are simple yet enlightening. He loves his treats, attention and cuddling time. Buddy teaches us how to keep perspective and maintain a positive outlook on life no matter what the situation may be.
—**Enrique G. Duprey**, DVM

Buddy the Beagle on Blueberry Street is a Must Read. Children will fall in love with this mischievous but lovable little beagle. Adults will also fall for the little guy as they get to see the world through his eyes. We watch him race in the dog derby, watch him deal with Blitz, a bully of a dog, and persevere with Buddy as he recovers from his accident. Buddy teaches us lessons about handling adversity and others. A delightful must read.
—**Sherri Stewart**, author,of *Liar, Liar, Pants on Fire*

In this delightful story, an older couple adopts a playful beagle and renames him Buddy, but they soon discover why the former owners named him Bandit. For along with a lot of doggy love, he also brings them a lot of doggy trouble. Author Debbie Burton does an excellent job of telling her story through the eyes of a loving and frisky beagle that just can't help getting into mischief. Anyone who loves dogs will laugh at his antics and smile at the affectionate bond between a dog and his owner.
—**Linda W. Rooks**, author of *The Bunny Side of Easter*

Buddy the Beagle on Blueberry Street

Debbie Burton

Copyright Notice

Buddy the Beagle on Blueberry Street

First edition. Copyright © 2019 by Debbie Burton. The information contained in this book is the intellectual property of Debbie Burton and is governed by United States and International copyright laws. All rights reserved. No part of this publication, either text or image, may be used for any purpose other than personal use. Therefore, reproduction, modification, storage in a retrieval system, or retransmission, in any form or by any means, electronic, mechanical, or otherwise, for reasons other than personal use, except for brief quotations for reviews or articles and promotions, is strictly prohibited without prior written permission by the publisher.

This book is a work of fiction. Characters are the product of the author's imagination. Any resemblance to actual events or persons, living or dead, is entirely coincidental.

Cover and Interior Design: Derinda Babcock

Editor(s): Derinda Babcock, Deb Haggerty

Illustrated By: Jenny Laskowski

Author Represented by WordWise Media Services

PUBLISHED BY: Elk Lake Publishing, Inc., 35 Dogwood Dr., Plymouth, MA 02360, 2019

Library Cataloging Data

Names: Burton, Debbie (Debbie Burton)

Buddy the Beagle on Blueberry Street / Debbie Burton

64 p. 216 mm × 140 mm (5.5 in × 8.5 in.)

Description: A rescue beagle finds a new home and a new name. His back is injured, but he learns to walk again.

Identifiers: ISBN-13: 978-1-950051-21-2 (trade) | 978-1-950051-22-9 (POD)

| 978-1-950051-23-6 (e-book.)

Key Words: Beagles, rescue dogs, dog training, back injuries in dogs, surgery for dogs, dog therapy, family2126

LCCN: 2019902596 Fiction

Dedication

For Herb, who always wanted a beagle.

Acknowledgments

Behind every author is a community of people who have contributed to the work. I wish to thank my husband, Herb, for his invaluable support. Herb inspired me to write a children's book, and stood by me through the process. Vickie Hudnall and Tracy Pratt spoke encouragement into my life from the beginning of my writing journey. Word Weavers Orlando took me under their wings and taught me the tools of the trade. Sherri Stewart provided an additional set of eyes and prompted me to not give up when I was ready to abandon the project. Jenny Laskowski brought Buddy's personality to life through her illustrations. Special thanks to my agent, Michelle S. Lazurek, and publisher, Deb Haggerty, for believing in me and the value of Buddy's message.

Table of Contents

Chapter One: A New Home, A New Name 1
Chapter Two: Who Needs People, Anyway? 3
Chapter Three: The Doggy Derby 7
Chapter Four: A Leap Of Fate 13
Chapter Five: The Hospital 19
Chapter Six: Yoga 23
Chapter Seven: New Friends 27
Chapter Eight: Christmas 31
Chapter Nine: Don't Give Up 35
Chapter Ten: Back To School 39
Notes 45
About the Author and Illustrator 47

Chapter One: A New Home, A New Name

Ding-Dong! Bandit raced to the front door with all the other dogs at the beagle rescue. *Who's at the door?*

Pat coaxed the dogs out of the living room and closed the doggy gate. Bandit pressed his nose between the rails. With his left paw, he scratched the metal gate. *Let me out.*

Pat opened the front door. A man and woman stood outside. "We're Henry and Jen Martin," the man said. "We called about adopting one of your beagles."

"Oh, yes, I remember." She motioned to the couple to come in. "You called about Bandit."

That's me. Here I am. He scratched the gate again.

Pat opened the gate just far enough to let the frisky dog in.

Hooray! He stood on his hind legs and pawed at Henry's jeans.

"Now that's no way to treat company," Pat scolded.

Henry reached down to pet the little beagle's head. "He's excited."

Bandit spun around and sniffed Jen's purse. *What's that smell?*

Jen grasped her purse in both hands and stepped away. "How long has he lived with you?"

"About two weeks," Pat said. "I'm already attached to the little guy. He has a way of stealing your heart. Maybe that's why he's called Bandit."

Henry knelt to read the information printed on his dog tag. "Bandit is an unusual name."

Pat picked up a stack of papers from the coffee table. "You can change his name if you want. He's young, and I'm sure he'll adjust. Why don't you two have a seat?"

Henry and Jen sat on the sofa. Bandit rested on the floor with his head on Pat's feet. His eyes darted back and forth between the two visitors.

Henry leaned forward. "He looks just like his picture."

Pat handed Henry the stack of papers. "These are Bandit's records. His first family didn't have time for him. His second owner died. He's only one year old and has already been through so much. Are you sure you want to adopt him?"

Henry shuffled through the papers. "I've wanted a beagle my whole life. What do you think, Jen?"

Jen peered into Bandit's eyes. "If you're willing to walk him, I'll agree. He's really cute, isn't he?"

Pat stood up from her chair. "Wonderful. I'm sure you want to get started. You have a long drive back to Orlando. He needs to go outside for a few minutes before you load him in the car."

Bandit ran outside for a romp in the yard. Max, his beagle friend, joined him.

"You're one lucky dog," barked Max. "I'm not sure you understand what's happening. You're being adopted. Your new family wants you to live with them. Make sure you obey their rules. If you don't, they might get rid of you."

"I'll try." *I wonder how successful I'll be. I'm a beagle. I follow my nose. Sometimes my nose gets me into trouble.*

Pat scooped Bandit up in her arms. "I'm going to miss you. Be good."

The little beagle licked Pat's face.

Henry attached a leash to his new dog's collar. He led him out to the car and placed him in his new crate. During the drive Henry and Jen talked.

"I don't like his name," said Henry. "Bandits steal things."

"You're right," Jen nodded. "We could be in for trouble. What do you want to name him?"

"I want to change his name to Buddy."

"That's a good idea," Jen agreed. "Buddy will be our buddy."

Bandit chewed the soft blanket inside his crate. *Buddy, what kind of a name is that? Not only do I have new owners, but they want to give me a new name. Not if I have anything to say about this. Max told me to listen and obey. This is going to be hard.*

Henry parked the car in the garage. He opened the crate and attached the leash to Bandit's collar. "Welcome to your new home, little guy. Meet your new neighborhood. We live on Blueberry Street."

Henry and Bandit began their first walk together. Bandit couldn't stop sniffing his new territory. *Hmm… I think a poodle has been around this tree. Oh, a spaniel squatted near this bush. Ah, my favorite smell, a garbage can must have fallen over on this driveway. But someone picked it up, of course. This area is full of interesting smells.*

After the walk, Henry opened the door to their house. Bandit raced around the kitchen and sniffed under the dining room table. *I can tell no kids live here. This floor is spotless. No leftovers, too bad.*

Then Bandit charged up the stairs, ran in the bedroom, and jumped on the bed.

Henry burst in. "Buddy, get down!"

Bandit cocked his head. *Buddy, who's Buddy? My name's Bandit, and I love jumping on beds.*

Henry lifted Bandit off the bed and carried him downstairs to the living room. Jen sat in her chair watching TV.

"Jen, can you keep an eye on this dog? I need to bring his crate inside."

"Sure. Hang on a sec. My phone is ringing." Jen rushed into the kitchen.

Bandit was alone. He raised his nose and sniffed the air. *Hmm … I smell peanut butter.* He jumped up on the chair and grabbed a peanut butter cookie from the side table. In record time, he gobbled the treat and leaped to the floor. *That was yummy.*

Jen returned to her chair and looked around for her cookie. Buddy licked his mouth and tried to look innocent. "So, now I understand why they named you Bandit."

The next day, Henry took Bandit in the backyard. "Let's play a game."

He tossed a ball and said, "Buddy, fetch."

Bandit's eyes followed the ball then scanned the yard for another dog. *Are you talking to me? I still don't know who you're talking to, but I've played this game before, so I'll fetch the ball.*

Bandit ran, picked up the ball and brought it back. Henry gave him a treat and said, "Good boy, Buddy."

Bandit wagged his tail. *Oh, I see. If I follow directions, I get a reward. Max would be proud of me. Maybe Buddy isn't such a bad name after all. I'll let him call me Buddy.*

For two days, Henry gave Buddy a treat whenever he answered to his new name. On the third day something changed.

"Buddy," Henry called.

Buddy rushed to Henry's feet. *Here I am.*

Henry reached down to give Buddy a pat instead of a treat. "Good boy."

Pats are almost as good as treats. Maybe he'll scratch behind my ears next time.

Chapter Two: Who Needs People, Anyway?

Jen's voice was loud and angry. "Buddy, did you chew on my favorite pen? Look at these teeth marks."

Buddy put on his are-you-talking-to-me look.

"I can see lines of blue ink around your mouth, so don't pretend."

Buddy lowered his head. *Uh-oh, I've been caught. I knew I should have buried that pen in the flowerbed.*

Later, Buddy's ear cocked when Jen complained to Henry. "Look at this. Buddy chewed the cover on my favorite book."

Buddy sniffed the book. *I call that dogeared.*

"I'm sorry, Jen. We need to dog proof our house like some people babyproof their homes. Nothing should be left within Buddy's reach. Remember, he's just a dog."

Just a dog? Buddy cocked his head to one side. *I thought I was your buddy.*

"Well." Jen folded her arms across her chest. "He's the one who needs to change, not us."

Henry reached for his phone. "I guess I need to call a dog trainer."

A few days later, the doorbell rang. Buddy barked. Henry opened the door, and a tall woman walked in.

"Miss Strict, I'd like you to meet Buddy."

He ran forward and raised his front paws, ready to pounce.

Miss Strict spoke in a firm voice. "Down, Buddy."

He lowered his paws to the floor and froze in a standing position.

Miss Strict gave him a treat.

He wagged his tail. *Yummy, I love salmon-flavored treats.*

Jen joined them in the living room. "We need your help. Buddy leaps onto the furniture. He jumps on guests and chews my books."

Buddy wanted to tell his side of the story. He barked. *Miss Strict, I'm not a bad dog. Look at me. I'm adorable. If you give me another salmon treat, I'll be quiet.*

To Buddy's surprise, Miss Strict grabbed his collar, pushed him into his crate, and shut the door. Buddy whined and pawed at the door. *Hey, let me out of here.*

Miss Strict ignored him. After Buddy settled down, she let him out. The three humans kept talking.

Then, Miss Strict turned to Buddy. "Good boy." She gave him another treat.

He cocked his head. *So, I get treats if I'm quiet?*

Buddy walked closer to Miss Strict and pawed at her foot. *How about one more?*

"No." Miss Strict returned Buddy to his crate.

Buddy sighed. *I think understand the rules of this new game.*

In a few minutes, Miss Strict let Buddy out of his crate. This time he sat near her and did not make a sound.

"Good boy." Miss Strict gave him one more treat. She stood up to leave.

Buddy sat still. She gave him his last treat.

"Thank you for coming," Jen said. "You've shown us what we need to do."

One night, Jen carried groceries in from the car. She left the back door open. The scent of grilled meat filled the air. Buddy couldn't resist and took off. He followed his nose into the neighbor's back yard.

He sniffed around the grill and lapped up some grease on the ground. Then, he looked toward the house. *The neighbor's back door is open. Why not check it out?*

Buddy sneaked inside. He threw back his head and howled. *I found the meat!*

The neighbor jumped back in surprise. "Hello, little guy. Where did you come from?"

Henry ran in. "I'm sorry, Bill. Buddy got out before we could catch him."

"He acts like a hunter who's cornered his prey. You've got quite a dog there."

"Yeah, a dog who needs to be taught a lesson."

"No problem. I'd like to take your dog hunting with me sometime."

Henry carried Buddy home. "You're a bad dog." He shoved him in his crate and slammed the door.

Buddy whined. *Henry, if I could speak human, I'd tell you to remember I'm a beagle. My parents were hunters, and I'm a hunter too. I bet I could live on my own if I had to. Who needs people, anyway?*

On New Year's Eve, Henry took Buddy for a walk. Boom! Boom! Buddy stopped in his tracks and whined. *What's that noise?*

Henry tugged on the leash. "Don't be afraid. Haven't you ever heard fireworks before?"

All of a sudden Buddy jerked and ran in the opposite direction. Henry dropped the leash.

"Stop!" He cried.

Buddy ran away. *I've got to get out of here. Where I can get away from those loud noises? My ears hurt.*

The loud booms continued.

"Come back." Henry raced after him but couldn't catch up.

Buddy raced across Blueberry Street. A car screeched to a stop just in time. The driver blew the horn. Buddy kept running.

Finally, Buddy stopped and looked around. *Where am I? This doesn't look like Blueberry Street. I'm tired. What should I do now? Where's Henry? Is he angry with me?* Buddy rested. He paused long enough for Henry to catch up.

"Buddy, look what I have."

He doesn't sound angry. Buddy walked to Henry and gobbled the treat from his outstretched hand.

Henry reached down and picked him up. "Time to go home, little buddy."

Henry carried him all the way back to Blueberry Street. The loud noises ended, and the neighborhood was quiet. *I like the quiet. I like how safe I feel in Henry's arms. I'm glad the loud noises stopped.*

Back in the house, Buddy licked Henry's hand and stepped into his crate. He curled up on the soft towel inside, ready to sleep. *Maybe I need people after all.*

Chapter Three: The Doggy Derby

Yum. Jen made bacon for breakfast. Buddy sniffed under the kitchen table in case a crumb dropped. *You two are way too neat when you eat.*

Henry opened the newspaper. "The Doggy Derby race is happening at the park on March third. Buddy can run fast. Let's sign him up."

"That's a great idea." Jen looked at the paper over Henry's shoulder. "We have time to get ready. Let's start training Buddy at the school playground where I used to teach. He can't run away because the area is fenced."

Buddy stopped sniffing and raised his head. *Run, did someone say run? Sign me up.*

Late that afternoon, the three of them drove to the school. Henry lifted Buddy out of his crate and hooked the leash to his collar. Jen opened the gate in the fence.

Henry and Buddy walked to one end of the yard. They turned around to face Jen, who stood in front of the closed gate. She waved Buddy's favorite squeaky toy.

He wagged his tail. *I love my rubber duck.*

"Buddy, come." Jen called.

Henry unfastened the leash.

The little beagle ran to Jen, but she didn't give him the duck. She gave him a treat instead. "Stay here."

Buddy obeyed. *This is different than playing fetch. All I do is run and I get a treat. Cool.*

Henry ran to meet them and gave Buddy a pat on the head. "Good boy."

He refastened the leash to Buddy's collar. Together they walked back to the starting place.

Jen squeezed the duck. *Squeak. Squeak.* She called Buddy again. He ran faster this time. *Does Jen have another treat?*

"Good boy, Buddy." She gave him a treat.

Henry joined them and attached Buddy's leash. "Well done, little guy."

The three of them walked to the car. Henry lifted Buddy into his crate. "We'll practice a few more times before the Doggy Derby."

Buddy wagged his tail. *Oh, so this is what the Doggy Derby is about—running and treats and family. I can't wait.*

The big day finally arrived. Henry, Jen, and Buddy joined the crowd of people and dogs in the park for the Doggy Derby. Buddy wagged his tail and sniffed. *Dogs, dogs everywhere. How fun.*

He followed his nose to a wonderful discovery. *Popcorn? What luck. Yummy.* He gobbled up a bite of the buttery treat when a deep growl sounded nearby.

A huge Doberman loomed over him and barked. His mean-looking eyes and sharp teeth scared Buddy. "That's my popcorn, you little runt. Go away."

Buddy trembled but stood tall and lifted his chin toward the big dog. "Finders keepers."

The Doberman strained on his leash and snarled.

"Blitz, stop," his owner yelled.

Henry pulled Buddy away before a fight started. *Blitz has a lot of nerve. That popcorn belongs to me. I was here first.*

Henry led Buddy to the check-in table where Jen waited for them.

"Buddy's in the middleweight group," she said.

"Good. He'll race against dogs his size."

Buddy peered up at Henry. *I'd rather race Blitz. I'm faster than him.*

Jen glanced at her watch. "Buddy will race in five minutes."

Henry nodded. "OK. Buddy and I will head toward the starting line. Take the duck and wait near the finish line for our turn."

Buddy watched two dogs at the starting line. A cute white poodle stood ready to race a scruffy gray terrier. Each of the owners held onto their pet's collar. A man blew a horn. Their owners let go of them, and they took off. The poodle ran half way but spun around and headed back to the starting place. The terrier stopped to greet some children standing at the side of the track. The crowd laughed. Both dogs' owners removed them from the racetrack.

Buddy edged closer to Henry. *Uh-oh, I hope I can do this. A crowd didn't watch me at the school playground when I practiced. Now the park is full of people who will all see me.*

The announcer called Buddy's name.

Henry crouched down with his hand on Buddy's collar. "When the horn blows, go to Jen."

Buddy looked to his left. In the next lane, a lean Italian greyhound sniffed the grass.

Buddy stretched in preparation. *I'm racing him? He looks fast, but I'm faster.*

The horn blew. Buddy took off. He ran straight to Jen and beat the greyhound by two seconds. The crowd cheered. Jen gave Buddy a treat and a big hug.

Henry met them at the finish line and attached Buddy's leash to his collar. "Way to go!"

Buddy panted. He lapped ice water at the drinking station.

"Attention, everyone," the announcer said, "This is the final race of the Doggy Derby. Buddy, the middleweight champion, will run against Blitz, the heavyweight champion."

Buddy froze. *What? Did he say Blitz?*

Henry drew Buddy close and knelt down, "Don't let Blitz scare you. He's just a bully. If you run fast, he'll never catch you."

"Well, well, well," growled Blitz as they took their places. "Hello, fast food eater. Let's see if you can run as fast as you eat."

Buddy scanned the other end of the track. *Ah, Jen's waiting for me. She has my toy.*

The horn blew. Buddy and Blitz took off. Buddy led until a squirrel darted across the track into a nearby grove of trees. His nose took over. He tracked the squirrel to the base of the nearest tree. The squirrel climbed high in the branches. The crowd laughed as Buddy stood at the base of the tree and howled. Henry and Jen came for him.

Uh-oh. They look angry.

Henry attached the leash to Buddy's collar and jerked him away from the tree. "Blitz won the Doggy Derby."

"Don't blame him, Henry. We never thought a squirrel would run across the course."

Buddy cocked his head and stared at the man holding his leash. *What's the matter, Henry? I'm a good boy. I tracked the squirrel, didn't I? Where's my treat?*

Jen patted Henry's arm. "Don't be upset. He's just a dog."

Buddy lowered his head. *Just a dog. I've heard that before. No treat this time.*

They passed the stage on their way out of the park. Blitz posed for pictures. He wore a shiny gold medal. The crowd cheered.

"This is the second year Blitz won the derby," said the announcer. "Congratulations, Doug, on your hard work as his trainer."

Doug stepped forward and shook the announcer's hand. Then Blitz and Doug left the stage.

"Henry reached out to shake Doug's hand. "Congratulations."

"Better luck next year," said Doug.

Henry shrugged. "Buddy's easily distracted."

"He's not distracted from food," Doug laughed.

"Buddy's a loser," Blitz barked.

Henry and Jen walked Buddy back to their house on Blueberry Street.

"Don't worry," said Jen. "There's always next year."

"Sure," mumbled Henry. "Next year."

Buddy looked up at Henry. *I'm sorry, Henry. I'll make this loss up to you. I promise I'll beat Blitz if you give me another chance.*

Chapter Four: A Leap of Fate

Summer passed quickly. Henry kept his promise to Jen. Every day, he got up early to walk Buddy. One morning, Henry picked up the pace. "Let's run, Buddy-boy."

They ran around the block together. *I haven't seen Blitz since the Doggy Derby. Wonder where he is? Why doesn't Henry run down the street where that Doberman lives?*

"Good boy. Keep running fast and you might beat Blitz next year."

Buddy wagged his tail. *Thanks, Henry. Don't give up on me.*

By the time they reached their front door, Buddy wanted a drink. He started to lick the sweat from Henry's leg.

"That tickles, Bud. Let's get some water."

Inside the house, Buddy lapped up the cool water from his dish and gulped his breakfast. *Delicious.*

Jen walked into the kitchen. "Can you believe Thanksgiving will be here soon? I'd like to paint the guest bedroom before our company comes."

Henry looked up from his cereal. "Whatever you think. Since you've retired from teaching, you have time. How will you keep Buddy out of the paint? We don't want any wet paw prints on the carpet."

"I'll keep the door to the bedroom shut."

Buddy licked the last crumbs from his bowl. *These humans sure talk a lot. I wish I understood all of their words besides "come, sit, stay, good dog, bad dog."*

A few days later, a new scent filled the house. Buddy followed the scent up the stairs to the bedroom. The door was open. Jen stood on a ladder with her back to him.

Buddy raised his nose and sniffed. *I think the smell is coming from the can on the table. The can is too high for me to reach.*

He turned his eyes toward the big bed in the middle of the room. *I haven't jumped on a big bed in a long time. Can I break the rules just this once? I'm fast. I can get up and down before Jen sees me.*

Buddy leaped up on the bed and back down again. He yelped. *Ow! Something popped in my back! Why do I have so much pain?*

Jen looked down. "Buddy, what are you doing here? I forgot to shut the door, didn't I?"

She climbed down from the ladder and picked him up. She carried him downstairs. Then she rushed back upstairs.

Buddy crawled to his bed. *Something's wrong. I can't walk very well.*

Henry walked in from work. "How was your day, Jen?"

"I think something's wrong with Buddy. He doesn't want to do anything but lie down, and he's trembling. Maybe he jumped off the bed when I painted the bedroom today."

Henry looked down at Buddy. "How did he get in the bedroom?"

"Uh … I forgot to close the door. I'm sorry. I feel terrible."

Henry hugged Jen.

Their little beagle whined. *I feel terrible, too. Can I have a hug?*

Henry sat down on the floor and stroked Buddy's ears. "It's already after six. Let's see how he is in the morning, then we'll call our vet."

The next morning, Buddy couldn't walk to the back yard. He couldn't even stand on all four feet. Henry carried him outside to go to the bathroom.

Buddy turned away from his breakfast. *I can't eat. I'm in too much pain.*

"I just got off the phone with Doctor Smiley," said Jen. "He wants to see Buddy."

Henry nodded. "Sure. I'll call my office and tell them I won't be in until later. Buddy's condition looks serious."

Henry carefully lifted Buddy into his crate, which he placed in the car. Jen got in the front seat. They drove to their vet's office nearby.

In the exam room, Doctor Smiley lifted Buddy out of his crate with gentle hands. "Poor little beagle."

He sat very still while the doctor examined him. *Doc, I wish I could speak human and tell you what's wrong. I feel miserable.*

"How long has Buddy been unable to move his hind legs?"

"Since this morning," said Jen. "His problem might have started when he jumped off the bed yesterday."

"Buddy needs a special x-ray to discover what's wrong with his back. I suggest you take him to Doctor Dee Pendable at the animal hospital. My nurse will call ahead to tell them you're coming."

Henry and Jen carefully placed Buddy's crate in the car. They drove through the busy Orlando traffic to the animal hospital. Then the couple carried him into the building.

A man greeted Henry and Jen in the reception area. "Hello, I'm Ted—one of the assistants here at the hospital. We've been expecting you. Please bring your dog into this waiting room. The doctor will be with you in a few minutes."

Soon, a lady with a white jacket came in. "I'm Doctor Dee Pendable, but most people call me Doctor Dee. How's your beagle? Tell me why you brought him to see me."

Jen started to cry. "Buddy can't walk. He hasn't acted normal since he jumped off the bed yesterday."

Henry put his arm around Jen. "Our dog's in so much pain he couldn't eat this morning."

"I'll x-ray his back and see what's going on," said Doctor Dee. "Please sign this paper before we begin. You were smart to keep him in his crate to avoid any further injuries."

Henry signed the paper.

Buddy whined. *I need help.*

Ted entered the room and carried Buddy to a room with a big machine. He placed him on a table and held him in one position. Buddy shivered. *Why is this room so cold?*

"Lie still, Buddy," said a lady. "We need to get two more pictures."

Buddy whined. *"I'm trying. This hurts."*

The lady patted Buddy's head. "That's a good boy."

Buddy relaxed. When they were finished, Ted put Buddy back in his crate and carried him to the room where Henry and Jen waited. The doctor walked in shortly after.

Buddy continued to whine. *Henry, they didn't solve my problem.*

Doctor Dee took a seat next to Henry and showed him the x-ray. "Just as I thought. Buddy shattered a disk in his back. Pieces of the disk are pressing on his spinal cord. That's why his hind legs are paralyzed. He needs to have surgery right away to remove the disk. Hopefully, he'll be able to walk again. We've had many cases like this, especially among beagles. Buddy will need to stay in the hospital for at least a week."

"Did the fall from the bed cause the problem?" Jen asked.

"I don't know for sure," said Doctor Dee. "Disk disease is passed down from adult dogs to their puppies. Buddy's landing might have put extra pressure on the disk. His spinal cord is bruised. I'll be honest, there's a chance he won't recover. He will need months of therapy. Are you willing to commit to providing the care he will need after surgery?"

Jen nodded as tears ran down her face.

Henry glanced at Jen, then his eyes moved to Buddy. "Absolutely."

Doctor Dee rose to her feet. "I'll call you about Buddy's condition tomorrow. You can visit him in two days."

Buddy's ears perked at his name. *What are they saying? What's all this talk?*

Henry opened the crate and patted Buddy's head. "Goodbye, my friend. Be brave. We love you."

Buddy whined again as Ted carried him away.

Chapter Five: The Hospital

Buddy opened his eyes and looked around. *Where am I? I'm not at home on Blueberry Street. I'm not in my own bed, and this is not my crate. How did I get in this cage, and who are those strange people in the room?*

He turned his head. Something stiff brushed the side of the cage. *Someone tied a plastic cone around my head. Why is a band wrapped around my front leg?*

Then he heard a voice. Doctor Dee stared down at him. "Oh, you're awake now. Are you hungry?"

Buddy cocked his head to one side. *How am I supposed to eat with a cone on my head?*

In a few minutes, a lady brought a bowl of wet dog food to his cage.

Buddy sniffed. *That smells good. I'm hungry. I didn't have breakfast today.*

The lady opened the door and scooped some of the dogfood out of the bowl with her hand. But she didn't take off the cone. "Here you go, little guy. My name is Tina. I'll be taking care of you."

Buddy licked the dogfood from her hand. *This is good. I'll be your friend forever.*

Across the room, Doctor Dee talked on her cell phone. "Buddy's awake now. The surgery went well. You can visit him Saturday. Have a nice Thanksgiving."

On Saturday, Tina wrapped Buddy in a small blanket. She carried him to the visiting room. As soon as they reached the doorway, Buddy sniffed. *Henry and Jen. Sorry, guys, I'm having troubling wagging my tail, but I'm really happy to see you. Are you going to take me home?*

Jen sat on the floor. Tina placed Buddy on her lap.

"Oh, Buddy. We've missed you terribly. We're so happy to see you."

"You look tired, little guy. I see you're sporting a new collar." Henry reached inside the plastic cone to pat his head.

Buddy's eyelids drooped. *I'm sleepy. This is a noisy place, but the food is good.*

Soon Doctor Dee came in. "Buddy's very weak. As you can see, we shaved the fur off his back. He has twelve stitches from the operation. He must wear a cone to make sure he doesn't pull them out with his teeth."

Buddy scratched at the plastic cone with his front paw. *I feel like a freak.*

Doctor Dee reviewed the notes in her file. "He should be able to go home next week. Once he is home, he needs six weeks of strict crate rest."

"Six weeks? If we can't walk him, how will Buddy use the bathroom?" Jen frowned.

"You'll need to carry him outside and then bring him right back in when he's finished. Buddy needs to wear doggy diapers for a while. He will have accidents."

Jen stroked Buddy's front paw. "We'll do whatever we can to help him get well. Thank you, doctor, for everything you've done."

The little beagle whined. *Doc, please tell them to take me home.*

Doctor Dee walked to the door. "Buddy will try to drag himself on his belly to get where he wants to go. Crawling will cause sores on his legs. He must be kept in his crate. Thank you for coming, but Buddy needs to rest now."

Tina lifted Buddy from Jen's lap.

Henry grasped Buddy's paw. "Be strong."

Buddy whined. *How am I supposed to rest in this place? The other dogs are always crying or barking. I want to go home.*

Late that night, after the other dogs calmed down, Buddy fell asleep. Max's face appeared to him in a dream, and he heard Max's voice. "Make sure you obey their rules. If you don't, they might get rid of you."

Buddy stirred and woke up. *I didn't follow the rules when I jumped on the bed. That's why I'm still here. Henry and Jen don't want me anymore.*

He started to cry.

Tina shined a light in his cage. "There, there, Buddy, don't cry."

She opened the door to pet his head. After a few minutes, he went back to sleep.

A few days later, Tina carried Buddy to the room where Henry and Jen waited.

Buddy wiggled with excitement. *Boy, am I glad to see you.*

When Tina lowered Buddy to the floor, he lost control of himself. A yellow puddle formed underneath him.

"Uh-oh." Jen stared at the puddle.

"Oh, I'm sorry. Buddy leaks." Tina pulled a paper towel from her pocket to dry the spot.

The door opened, and Doctor Dee walked in. "We've enjoyed having Buddy with us, but we're releasing him today. Before you leave, I want to show you an exercise to help Buddy's hind legs get stronger. First, he must learn how to stand again."

Doctor Dee slid a rolled bath towel under Buddy's belly. She gently lifted his hind legs to a standing position. Tina positioned herself directly in front of him. She held a treat just out of his reach.

Buddy stared at the treat. *I'm ready to do whatever you say.*

Doctor Dee removed the towel. Buddy's hind legs dropped to the floor. She repeated the exercise. Buddy stood for two seconds this time. Tina gave him the treat.

Doctor Dee let Buddy relax. "If you do this exercise four times a day, Buddy will get stronger and stand for longer periods. Only give him the treat if he stands on all four paws."

Tina showed Henry and Jen how to diaper Buddy.

Buddy whined. *I hope Blitz doesn't see me like this. I'm not a baby.*

"I'll need to see him back in one week to remove the stitches." Doctor Dee handed Jen a prescription. "Buddy will need to take pain medicine."

Jen made the appointment at the front desk and joined Henry and Buddy in the car.

Buddy tried to get comfortable inside his crate. *I hate wearing this silly cone. At least I'm going home.*

Henry started the engine. "I can't believe our poor dog needs to stay in his crate for six weeks. We must follow a schedule to make sure we give him his medicine and do the exercises."

"We'll do our best, Henry. I have hope he will get better."

"His healing is going to take a long time."

Jen fastened her seatbelt. "I'm glad we have each other, and I'm really glad we have Buddy."

Buddy gave a sigh of relief. *I'm glad I've got another chance.*

Chapter Six: Yoga

Buddy yawned from inside his crate. *I'm bored.*
Henry walked into the room. "Jen, we need to take Buddy out."
"Let's use my old yoga mat. He'll be more comfortable while he exercises."
Henry lifted Buddy's crate. "Good idea. We can change his diaper outside too, so we won't have a mess in the house."
When all the supplies were ready, Henry opened the crate and placed Buddy on the yoga mat.
The outdoor smells tingled Buddy's nose. *I've got to move.*
Since he wasn't wearing a leash, he was free. Buddy slid on his belly into the grass. Then he crawled forward by pulling with his front feet and dragging his hind legs. *Wow! This is fun. I don't hurt anymore. Is this how a snake crawls?*
Henry grabbed him. "You must stay on the mat."
"I don't think Buddy knows his hind legs aren't working." Jen sat down on the front steps. "He still wants to run."
Henry held Buddy tight. "We can't let him do that. He'll get sores on his legs if he drags himself."
They worked together to exercise Buddy's hind legs.
Bill, the next-door neighbor, peered over the hedge. "Are you doing yoga with Buddy?"
Henry looped his fingers through Buddy's collar. "Long story, Bill. A broken disk in Buddy's back pressed on his spinal cord. His spinal cord was bruised, and his hind legs are paralyzed. Two weeks

ago, he had surgery. We're doing exercises to help him stand. The doctor said he might walk again if we follow her instructions. I sure hope she's right."

"That's tough. I'm sorry Buddy can't walk. He's such a cute little dog. Hope he gets better." Ted opened his door and went inside.

Henry lowered his voice. "I hope I don't have to keep telling Buddy's story to everyone who comes along."

"Me too." Jen nodded.

Henry and Jen worked with Buddy on the mat. They practiced helping him stand. Then they stretched and rubbed his hind legs. As Jen changed his diaper, Buddy heard someone approach. He lifted his head off the mat.

"Lie still, Buddy." Jen scolded, as she finished putting the diaper in place.

Buddy squirmed. *I can't lie still. I smell Blitz. I have to get up.*

Soon Blitz and Doug loomed over the low hedge.

"Look at that," barked Blitz. "The baby beagle is wearing diapers."

Buddy lowered his head inside the cone. *What could be worse than this? Not only am I wearing a diaper, I have a cone on my head. How embarrassing.*

Henry curled his fingers through Buddy's collar and held on tight.

Buddy twisted and turned. *Let me up. Blitz needs to be taught a lesson. Let me at him.* "I'm not a baby," he barked.

Doug pulled his dog back from the hedge. "Easy, Blitz."

Henry pinned Buddy to the mat while Jen stepped closer to Doug. "Buddy injured his spine, and he's paralyzed. He had surgery, and we want to help him walk again. For now, he needs to wear a diaper."

Doug shook his head. "A dog in diapers is no fun."

"You're telling me." Henry glanced at Buddy's crate. "He's supposed to have six weeks of crate rest, and he might not be able to walk for months."

"What a shame, Henry. I'm sure you realize Buddy might not run in the next Doggy Derby."

"Serves him right," Blitz growled. "That little bandit stole my popcorn."

"Dude, that's history," barked Buddy. "Get over it."

"Jen, I think we'd better take Buddy in now. See you later, Doug."

"Time for the baby to take his nap," snarled Blitz. Doug pulled Blitz back and they walked on.

Once they were out of earshot, Henry turned to Jen. "I'm afraid Doug is right. Buddy won't be in the next derby. He has a bigger challenge now, just learning to walk again."

Jen gathered their supplies. "Don't worry. The doctor said Buddy might get better. We can't give up hope."

Henry picked Buddy up and carried him inside. Buddy let out a sigh. *Jen's right, I won't give up. I want to beat Blitz at the next derby. I'll show him.*

A few days later, Henry and Jen took Buddy back to the animal hospital to get his stitches removed. The three of them waited in the exam room.

Buddy peered through the door of his crate at Henry. *You better not have any ideas about leaving me here. This cone is driving me crazy. I need some good news today.*

Soon Tina and Doctor Dee walked in. "How are the exercises going?"

Henry stood up to stretch. "My back aches and my knees are sore from working with Buddy on a yoga mat."

"Yoga mat?" asked the doctor.

"Her idea." Henry pointed at Jen.

Doctor Dee washed her hands. "Try using a card table in a corner of the room when you work with him. Then Buddy can't run. Cover the card table with a towel so his feet won't slide."

Henry nodded. "Good idea. Why didn't I think of that?"

Tina held Buddy still while the doctor removed his stiches. Buddy sighed. *Ah ... that feels better. Those stiches were itchy.* Doctor Dee removed the cone and patted Buddy's head. He licked her hand. *Thanks, Doc. You've made my day. That's one less thing Blitz can laugh at me about. Now, let's talk about this diaper.*

The doctor returned Buddy to his crate. "Now that Buddy's stitches are out, he can begin water therapy. We've had great success with the underwater treadmill. If you can manage, I'd like him to come to therapy twice a week."

"Yes," said Jen. "I can bring him. We'll start on Monday."

"Great," Doctor Dee continued, "Nurse Hope, our physical therapist, will meet you at the front desk."

Buddy looked up at Jen. *Water therapy? Is that like taking a bath? I don't like baths.*

Chapter Seven: New Friends

Jen and Buddy arrived at the hospital early Monday morning for water therapy. Jen lifted Buddy out of the car and carried him through the front door.

"May I help you?" asked the receptionist.

"Yes. Buddy has an appointment for water therapy."

Buddy pressed his head against Jen's neck. *Anything but a bath.*

A cheerful young lady greeted them. "Hello, Jen, I'm Nurse Hope. I've read Buddy's record, and I'm so happy to meet him. I'll need to work with him alone. If a pet is in therapy and his owner is present, he won't work as hard. Can you wait here? Each session will take an hour."

Jen nodded. "That's fine. I brought a book to read."

"Come with me, little guy." Nurse Hope carried Buddy to the therapy room. She placed him on a table.

Buddy looked around. *I'm scared. Is Jen going to leave me here again?*

Nurse Hope spoke calmly to him as she massaged his hind legs. Buddy relaxed and licked her hand. *I could get used to this.*

"Aw, thanks for the doggy kiss." Nurse Hope attached a leash to his chest harness so he couldn't crawl away. Her helper placed Buddy's hind legs in a sling. Nurse Hope held the leash in her left hand and grasped the straps to the sling in her right. She lifted Buddy's hind legs off the ground. "Let's go for a walk."

Buddy whined. *I can't. Don't you know I can't walk?*

Nurse Hope's helper opened the door, and Buddy sniffed the air. *Hmm...new smells.*

She lifted his hind legs, and Buddy stepped forward with his front feet. He could move on two feet instead of four.

Buddy sniffed again, and his front feet walked faster. *I can't believe I'm actually going somewhere. This is fun.*

After their walk around the hospital grounds, Nurse Hope led Buddy back inside the hospital. She took off the sling and placed a rolled towel under his belly. She held the ends of the rolled towel in each hand and raised him to a standing position. Her helper opened the door to a glass pen and coaxed Buddy inside with a treat. Then Nurse Hope shut the door.

Buddy lifted his head and whined. *What's going to happen now?*

Warm water started pouring in through the floor. The water got deeper and was soon up to his belly. Buddy whined louder. *This is scary. I've never had a bath like this before.*

Nurse Hope continued to hold the rolled-up towel around Buddy's stomach. Buddy stood still. The floor rolled. Buddy had to move with the motion. He stepped forward with his front feet. His back feet followed. Nurse Hope removed the towel.

Buddy gazed up at Nurse Hope. *Maybe there's hope for me yet. The water is holding me up. I can walk!*

"Good job, Buddy, keep going," Nurse Hope cheered.

After a minute, Buddy slowed down. *I've walked and walked, but the scenery still looks the same.*

The floor stopped rolling and the water drained out. Nurse Hope picked Buddy up and dried him with a towel. "Good boy, Buddy. Did you like the underwater treadmill?"

Buddy licked her hand again.

"I think that means you did. That's all for today. Every time you use the treadmill, you'll grow stronger."

Nurse Hope wrapped Buddy in a dry towel and carried him out to Jen in the waiting room. "Buddy walked on the underwater treadmill for one minute."

Jen held Buddy close. "That's great. I'm so proud of you."

Just then, a man walked through the front door carrying a small beagle.

"Hi, Keith." Nurse Hope waved. "I'll be back in a minute. I need to clean the treadmill."

Nurse Hope excused herself and returned to the therapy room.

Buddy took a deep whiff in the other dog's direction. He loved her scent. *Wow, she's pretty.*

Jen was interested too and introduced herself. "Hi, I'm Jen, and this is Buddy. Is your beagle friendly?"

"Yes, this is Daisy." Keith gave the two dogs an opportunity to sniff each other's noses.

"You're sweet," whimpered Buddy.

Daisy leaned closer. "You have such big brown eyes."

"Is Daisy here for therapy, too?" asked Jen.

"Yes. She suffered from a back injury three months ago. She was paralyzed, but now she's starting to walk. I'm her keeper. Daisy's employed by a local hotel."

"Employed?" asked Jen.

Keith nodded. "Daisy sniffs out bedbugs in hotel rooms. She's a very valuable employee. Since her surgery, she's not been able to work. The owners of the hotel are looking forward to her return."

"That's amazing. I'm glad she's doing better. This is Buddy's first day in therapy."

Nurse Hope came back into the waiting room. "Aw, the two beagles look so cute together. I'm ready now."

"Goodbye." Buddy sniffed Daisy again. "Let's be friends."

Daisy yipped. "Hang in there, Buddy, you'll walk again."

Nurse Hope carried Daisy to the therapy room, and Jen carried Buddy to the car.

"How do you like that? We met a bed-bug-sniffing beagle."

Buddy licked Jen's hand. *I like her a lot.*

Chapter Eight: Christmas

Henry laced up his sneakers. "I'm going for a run."

Buddy stirred inside his crate. *I used to run with Henry, but not anymore. I've been going to therapy twice a week for three weeks, but I can only walk in water. I hate my life.*

"When I get back, we'll decorate our tree. I can't believe Christmas is almost here."

Jen looked up from her book. "Let's set the tree near Buddy. He must be getting bored."

Buddy scratched his crate door. *Bored? Did someone say bored? You don't know what bored means until you've lived in box for a month.*

Later, the family gathered in the living room. Henry set up the tree next to the TV. From his crate, Buddy watched them string the lights. *Can I help? I'd like to get my paws on those lights.*

Jen opened a box and hung a candy cane on the tree.

Buddy whined. *I want out of here. Can you at least toss one of those candy canes my way?*

"I'm sorry but we can't let you out now." Henry picked up the remote and turned on the TV. "I wish Buddy could walk."

A commercial flashed on the screen. Jen turned around. "Look, there's a dog with his bottom strapped to a little cart. He can run using his front paws."

Buddy lifted his head. *Am I too late to write Santa Claus? I've always wanted my own wheels.*

"Sounds like they gave up," said Henry. "If we did that, I don't think Buddy would ever walk."

Buddy lowered his head and sighed. *That's right, Henry. I don't deserve wheels. After all, I broke the house rules.*

"Let's believe for the best," said Henry. "Maybe Doctor Dee will have some good news when the six weeks of crate rest is finished."

Buddy stirred inside his crate. *Sounds like Henry and Jen are awake.*

Henry walked into the kitchen. "Good morning, Buddy. Time for your exercises."

Jen yawned as she walked through the kitchen door. "Exercises? Do we have to do exercises now? We don't get a break for Christmas?"

"Come on, Jen. We promised Doctor Dee we would follow her orders. Working with Buddy isn't so bad, now that we set up the card table in the garage."

Jen sighed. "OK. Let's go."

As they did every morning, Jen held the treat in front of Buddy while Henry lifted him to the standing position. "Buddy!" Jen gasped. "You wagged your tail."

"Amazing. You haven't wagged your tail since the accident." Henry put his arms around Buddy's neck.

Buddy licked Henry's face. *I don't know what I did right, but I like you guys too.*

"I can't wait to tell Nurse Hope." Jen gave Buddy two treats. "What a wonderful Christmas."

The day after Christmas, Jen drove Buddy back to the hospital for therapy.

"How was your holiday?" asked Nurse Hope.

"Great. Buddy wagged his tail on Christmas morning."

"That's wonderful. His spinal cord is healing. Messages are moving from his brain to his tail."

"When will the messages move to his back feet?"

"That takes a lot longer." Nurse Hope lifted Buddy from Jen's arms. "Let's go to work."

Two weeks later, Jen took Buddy for a checkup with Doctor Dee.

"Buddy's crate rest is finished. Now that he can stand on his own, he can stay in an exercise pen at home."

"What do you mean?"

Doctor Dee showed her a picture. "Buddy needs to be in a small fenced-in space, kind of like a playpen. Then he can stand up but not crawl around in the house."

Buddy cocked his head. *A pen? I chewed on a pen once, and I got in trouble.*

"Buddy doesn't need to wear diapers anymore. He can go for longer walks. Put his hind feet in a sling like Nurse Hope uses. You can order one online."

"Thanks for the good news, Doctor Dee. I can't wait to tell Henry."

Buddy wagged his tail. *What? No more diapers? Yay! I'm a big boy now.*

Chapter Nine: Don't Give Up

The doorbell rang. Henry opened the front door and brought a huge box into the kitchen. "Jen, Buddy's exercise pen is here."

Buddy strained his neck to see out of his crate. *What's that?*

Jen hurried downstairs. "Great, I can't wait to see."

Henry opened the box and fastened the metal pieces together to build the walls. He placed the pen in one corner of the kitchen. "I think this corner will be a good place. If we have the door of the pen near the outside exit, Buddy won't need to travel very far."

Jen picked up the wrapping on the floor. "Hopefully, Buddy won't have too many accidents on the way out. I don't want to make him wear diapers again."

Buddy lowered his head. *Diapers? Don't mention that word ever again.*

"We need to keep Buddy on a schedule for his walks." Henry practiced opening and closing the door to the pen. "Let's limit the amount of water he drinks. Doctor Smiley said sixteen ounces of water a day should be enough for a dog his size."

Jen placed Buddy's dog bed in the pen, along with a throw rug for him to stand on.

Buddy pawed at the crate door. *Hey, am I going to get out of here now?*

Henry lifted Buddy out of his crate and into the pen.

Buddy nestled into the bed he hadn't slept in for six weeks. *This is so comfortable. I feel like I'm really home.*

Henry carried Buddy to the garage to prepare him for his walk. He placed his back legs in the sling. Then he attached the leash to his harness. "This is a lot of work, Jen. I need both of my hands to move Buddy down the street."

"I'm coming too." She picked up the poop bags.

Buddy wagged his tail. *I love our walks, because Henry does most of the work. I take care of the front and he handles the back end.*

"Everybody's staring at us, Henry. I guess our neighbors have never seen a dog in a sling."

Henry didn't look around. "Let them stare. I'm busy."

One evening, the three of them crossed Doug's path. Blitz pulled hard on his leash. Doug strained to keep control of him.

"Who do we have here?" barked Blitz. "Buddy, the little puppet. I'm going to name you Pinocchio."

"Leave me alone, Blitz. I'm improving. At least I'm not in diapers anymore," Buddy growled.

Henry steered Buddy in the opposite direction, away from Blitz.

"Sorry," Doug called out. "You surprised us."

Henry, Jen, and Buddy walked on.

"Blitz really irritates Buddy."
You got that right, Henry.
Henry glanced over his shoulder. "I think they're gone now."
Jen stared after Blitz and Doug. "If I see them coming, I'll warn you, and we can walk a different way."
"Sometimes bullies need to be stood up to, but not now. We must protect Buddy. We don't want a big dog like Blitz to jump on him. He'll get hurt again."

During the next two months, Buddy continued his physical therapy sessions with Nurse Hope. Although he walked on the underwater treadmill, he still couldn't walk on land without the sling. Nurse Hope came up with an idea.

"Let's try this, Buddy-boy." She slid a narrow strap under his belly to give his body some support. His back feet touched the ground, and he had greater freedom of movement. The strap worked like a safety net. If Buddy's hind legs dropped, Nurse Hope could raise him to a standing position again.

During their walk around the hospital grounds, Buddy's hind legs collapsed. *I quit.*

Nurse Hope pulled up on the strap. "Get up, Buddy."

Buddy lowered his head. *I can't. I don't think I'll ever get better. They might as well send me back to the rescue.*

Then Buddy sniffed a familiar scent. *Ah, Daisy, the pretty beagle I met a few weeks ago. She's with her nurse, and she can walk on all four paws.*

Buddy focused on pushing his hind legs to a standing position. *I've got to try ...*

"Way to go, Buddy," yipped Daisy.

Nurse Hope gave him a treat. "Looks like Daisy will be going back to work at the hotel soon."

Daisy sniffed closer to Buddy's side and yipped. "You're adorable. Don't give up."

Daisy thinks I'm adorable. He wagged his tail and walked all the way back to the hospital.

Chapter Ten: Back to School

Nurse Hope opened the door to the treadmill tank. She picked Buddy up and dried him with a towel.

Buddy shook off the extra water. *Time to go home. I smell Jen. She must be nearby.*

Jen read a book while she waited for him. He padded into the room at Nurse Hope's side and wagged his tail. *Look at me, Jen.*

"We had a great session today." Nurse Hope smiled when Jen looked up.

Jen stared at the nurse's empty arms. "Where's Buddy?"

"Right here." She pointed.

"Buddy! You walked in here."

I like Jen's happy voice.

"Instead of using the sling, walk Buddy with this skinny strap. The strap gives his back some support and allows him to use his hind legs."

Jen reached down to pet Buddy's soft ears. "You walked. I'm so proud of you."

Buddy licked Jen's hand. *Thanks to Daisy, I didn't give up.*

Nurse Hope gave two red booties to Jen. "Buddy will need to wear latex booties. He doesn't lift his back feet correctly when he walks. I don't want him to get sores from dragging those feet on the sidewalk. You can order more online. He needs a size small."

"Thanks, nurse. You've done an amazing job with Buddy."

Buddy the Beagle on Blueberry Street

The next day, Henry and Jen walked down Blueberry Street with Buddy. Jen picked up a flyer someone dropped. She read, "The Doggy Derby is this Saturday." She looked at Henry. "Has a year already passed?"

Henry glanced at the flyer. "Too bad we can't enter Buddy. He can walk with the strap under his belly, but he can't walk by himself. Running is out of the question."

Buddy's tail drooped. *I'm sorry, Henry, but I'm trying my best. I know I'm not ready to beat Blitz. You might as well send me back to the rescue.*

They came to a house a few doors down where a new family moved in. Two little boys played in the front yard.

"Look—a doggy wearing shoes," said the younger boy.

"Can we pet him?" asked the older one.

"Sure," said Jen. "His name is Buddy."

"Aw, he licked my hand," the little boy squealed.

The older boy stroked Buddy's ears. "I like his red shoes."

Buddy wagged his tail. *Thanks. Okay, go ahead. You can tell me. I'm adorable.*

Just then, their mother walked out on the front porch. "Look at the adorable beagle."

Buddy wagged his tail. *See, Henry, I may not be able to run, but everyone loves me.*

The next day, Henry shared an idea with Jen. "Let's take Buddy to the schoolyard where we taught him how to run. Maybe he can practice walking there."

"Great idea. He'll be safe with no other dogs around."

They loaded Buddy into the car and drove to the school. Henry lifted him out of his crate and led him to the fence.

Buddy sniffed around the gate. *I remember this place. This is where we practiced for the Doggy Derby.*

Jen opened the gate, and the three of them walked in.

"This time, let's position ourselves closer together," said Henry. "I want Buddy to walk. If there's a lot of space between us, he might try to run. He's not ready for that yet."

Jen stood ten feet away from Henry. He dropped the skinny strap and unfastened the leash from Buddy's chest harness.

"Come, Buddy," Jen called and held out a treat.

Buddy walked on all four paws to Jen.

"Good boy," Henry shouted.

"Hooray!" Jen gave Buddy his treat.

Buddy wagged his. *I can't wait to show Blitz I can walk again.*

He walked back and forth between Jen and Henry a few more times.

"Okay, Jen. We'd better give him a rest. Let's go home."

Two weeks later, Buddy started walking without the strap for longer distances. However, the day for the Doggy Derby came and went, and Henry did not sign Buddy up to race.

Jen continued to drive him for therapy with Nurse Hope. One day in April, she gave Jen some good news. "Buddy doesn't need to come for therapy anymore. He's walking on his own one hundred percent of the time."

Jen was so happy she cried. "Thank you, Nurse Hope. Buddy never would have walked again without your help."

"You and Henry worked hard too."

Buddy wagged his tail. *Don't forget me. This wasn't easy, you know.*

A few days later, a large black figure approached them as they walked on Blueberry Street.

"Henry, is that Blitz?" Jen whispered.

"I think so. Doug is with him."

Buddy froze. *Blitz? Did someone say Blitz?*

"Should we turn around?" Jen stared at the figures as they approached.

"No. Sometimes bullies need to be stood up to."

The three of them continued walking toward Blitz and Doug.

Buddy peered up at Henry. *Don't worry, I'm not afraid.*

Doug and Henry stopped at the same time. Blitz and Buddy stood by their masters, staring at each other.

Doug told Blitz to stay and gave him a treat.

Henry told Buddy to stay and gave him a treat.

Doug spoke first. "I can't believe Buddy is walking."

"We believed in him and never gave up. By the way, did Blitz win the Doggy Derby this year?" asked Henry.

Doug ran his fingers through his hair. "The craziest thing happened. During the final race, a squirrel ran across the track. Blitz gave chase just like Buddy did last year. He lost, and now I'm trying to live down my embarrassment."

Blitz lowered his head.

"Looks like we have something in common," yipped Buddy. "We were both led astray by a squirrel. Did you catch that fur ball?"

"No," Blitz answered. "The little rascal was faster than me."

"That's a shame. You lost the squirrel and the race," Buddy smiled his doggy smile.

Blitz wagged his stubby tail. "I'm sorry I made fun of you, Buddy. You're a nice guy and a dedicated athlete."

Buddy spied a piece of popcorn lying by the side of the road. He strained on his leash and grabbed the treat.

"What are you doing?" Henry grasped the leash.

Buddy approached Blitz and dropped the popcorn at his feet. "I'm sorry you lost. I should have shared the popcorn with you on the day I raced. You deserve this."

"Well, I never …"-Doug's mouth dropped open.

Blitz gobbled the popcorn. "Thanks."

Then, the two dogs sniffed each other.

"By the way, congratulations." Blitz yipped, "You can walk again."

Buddy yipped back. "Thanks, I may not win a race, but I'm happy to win your respect."

"Buddy, you're amazing," said Doug.

Henry reached down to pet Buddy's ears. "He sure is amazing. I wouldn't trade him for anything."

Buddy wagged his tail. *I'm here to stay.*

Blitz howled for everyone in the neighborhood to hear, "Buddy the Beagle, champion of Blueberry Street."

Notes

Questions for Discussion regarding *Buddy the Beagle on Blueberry Street:*

1. Buddy learned never to give up. Are you facing a challenge? What steps could you take to not give up? How can we encourage others not to give up?
2. Buddy had trouble following rules. Why are rules important? Which rules do you have trouble following in your house?
3. Do you think Buddy learned that he really did need people? Who did Buddy need?
4. Blitz bullied Buddy on more than one occasion. Do you agree with Henry's statement that sometimes we need to stand up to bullies? How did Blitz change at the end of the story?
5. Who was the real champion in this story? Why?

The Doggone Truth

Buddy's surgery and recovery really happened. In November 2013, the author's pet beagle, Buddy, suffered from a ruptured disk in his back. Degenerative disk disease is a common hereditary condition among beagles. Buddy's recovery from paralysis took four months. The author wishes to thank Corrine Drive Animal Hospital of Orlando, and Affiliated Veterinary Specialists, P.A. of Maitland, Florida, for their medical expertise and support.

About the Author

Award winning poet Debbie Burton began writing after she retired from teaching. Her poems have appeared in issues of *Time of Singing Literary Journal* and *Refresh Bible Study Magazine*. Debbie is a member of Word Weavers International. She serves as a volunteer in the Read2Succeed program of Orange County Public Schools. Debbie enjoys camping in her home state of Florida with her husband Herb and their sweet beagle, Buddy. Visit the author at https://debbieburton.blog. Readers can also follow Debbie and Buddy at https://www.facebook.com/buddyfanclub.

About the Illustrator

Jenny Laskowski is an artist and illustrator based out of Tampa, Florida. She earned her BFA from the University of South Florida. In addition to working as a studio artist, Jenny teaches art to middle schoolers. She enjoys spending time with her husband, Steven, and their two cats, TomJohn and Thursday. To learn more about Jenny visit her at https://www.jenopee.com.

Made in the USA
Columbia, SC
12 March 2019